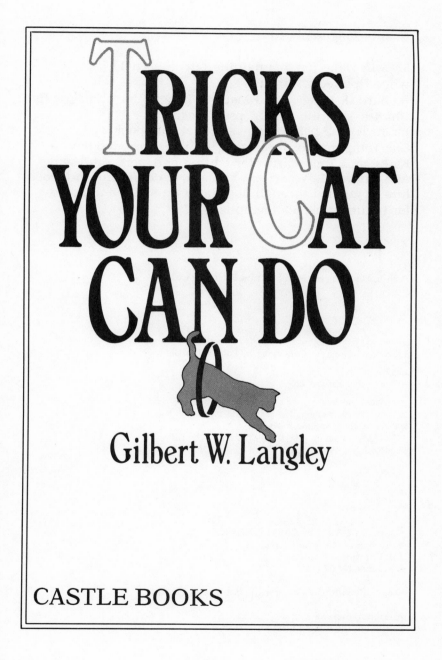

# TRICKS YOUR CAT CAN DO

## Gilbert W. Langley

CASTLE BOOKS

## Acknowledgments to

My wife Jane for maintaining our household
while I played with cats
Richard J. Langley and Maurice Langley for photography
Charles McBride, Ph.D., psychologist,
for reviewing behavioral aspects of this book
Gay Tompkins for assistance with the introduction
Kathy and Tom Martin for editing and word processing
And, above all, Weaver, my cat, who patiently and with good
humor jumped through hoops, sat on stools and posed
for innumerable photographs

Published by arrangement with Sterling Publishing Co., Inc.


**Library of Congress Cataloging in Publication Data**
Langley, Gilbert W.
  Tricks your cat can do.

  Includes index.
  Summary: Instructions for general cat training
and for teaching specific tricks.
  1. Cats—Training. [1. Cats—Training]. I. Title.
SF446.6.L36  1985    636.8'08'87    84-26768

Originally published by Sterling Publishing Co., Inc.

ISBN 1-55521-755-9

# Contents

*To Jean*

# Feline Follies

There are many myths about cats. The mysterious "air" of the cat has resulted in a rich history of superstition and religion, folklore and old husbands' tales. Cats were worshipped in ancient Egypt; regarded as the evil companions of witches in Europe, during the Middle Ages. To this day, there are those who believe that cats kill newborn infants.

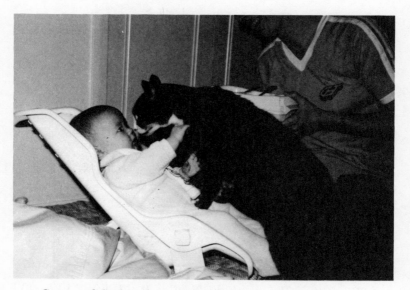

*Cat and baby discussing foolish superstitions.*

Cats are independent. People don't own cats; cats own people. Try this recipe: Take independence and add to it a bit of serenity, a pinch of tranquillity and lots of physical grace. Look deeply into a cat's eyes and see reflections of your own soul. This is the recipe mix that has convinced generations that the cat is a creature of strange instincts—untrainable and obstinate.

*Some cats start by ignoring you in the hope that you will forget the whole idea.*

*Other cats seem almost eager to learn.*

The myth will continue, but . . . for centuries, cats have been performing tricks under the big top. (Big cats, ferocious cats!) Spectators have been enthralled by the cats' strength and beauty, and the trainer's ability to avoid being eaten. By applying a few simple training techniques and using basic principles of behavior modification, you can take cat stunts out of the circus and put them into your living room.

Physically the differences between the structure of the human brain and that of the cat is one of degree rather than kind. Cat behavior is not arbitrary or a result of some freak chance of fate. There are reasons for its occurrence. Cats respond to their environment and reinforcement just as you or I do.

A perfect example of a cat's response to environmental stimuli probably occurs at your house at least twice a day. Turn on the electric can opener or open the refrigerator door and watch your cat appear magically

*You will find that training your cat can be child's play.*

10

from nowhere. Your cat could be in stage five of sleep, having an out-of-body experience, yet this sound will cause it—in seconds—to gain its feet and spin its wheels to propel its furry self into the kitchen.

So here's your chance to help your poor cat, who has been left unemployed by the onslaught of better mousetraps, to again have a chance to "earn its keep" and regain a sense of pride and self-esteem. Yes, that distant cousin of the tiger, your boarder, the domestic quadruped that has plagued your life by eating your plants and tearing a five-inch hole in the couch, can now be taught to perform interesting tricks to impress your friends and neighbors.

You, as the trainer, will enjoy satisfaction at acquiring a degree of control over nature and your household. And who knows? When you consider how many cats earn large sums of money as performers perhaps your charmer can earn enough to pay for some of the household furnishings it has demolished. So send the family to the basement or the movies, get in some fish or other cat treats and prepare to conquer Nutley (or Dexter, or Thunder or Mi-Mi).

# TECHNIQUES

# Basic Principles

An understanding of a few principles underlying the learning process will aid you in training your cat and can even be applied to other important people in

*Once you've mastered the principles in this chapter, you can get important people to jump through hoops for you.*

your life. If you are a parent, perhaps you can transfer some of what you learn to teach your child to respond appropriately to a stimulus (you) and—at the least—get him or her to pick up and put away toys. Now, that would be an impressive trick!

*Actually, to get a cat to jump through a hoop is a lot easier than to get a child to put away toys.*

The beauty of behavior modification is that it bypasses all of those complicated psychoanalytical processes. Behavior modification is a method of changing and shaping new behavior. It is based on a set of principles derived from laboratory experiments with animals. These principles have been found to work in a wide range of settings.

Behavior modification differs from doing "what comes naturally" in that a program for dealing with behavior has been developed, as opposed to the usual

*The number of things a cat can be trained to do is surprising; driving a car, however, is not one of them.*

haphazard series of events. If, without a plan, you take your cat (after it has been fed) into the distraction-filled family living room to teach him tricks, you are bound to fail. Your cat isn't going to be thrilled either. You could feed him his favorite food, and he still would not perform.

By using some of the principles laid out here, however, your chances for success are improved enormously.

"*Nothing in front, nothing behind. Where are the treats?*"

## BEHAVIOR

To understand how to modify behavior, let's start by understanding what it is.

Behavior is an observable action. Observable is the key word. If two sane, sober people see the same event their descriptions should be nearly identical. Nothing is guessed at. We do not talk about motives which may have caused the behavior. We are only interested in the action itself when we discuss behavior.

In short, what we want to do in teaching our cat tricks is to establish some degree of control over his actions.

*Understanding a cat's behavior is not always easy.*

To establish this control, certain conditions have been shown to be best. One is that the training should be described in operational terms so that everyone's definition of events is the same. An analysis of behavior in a trained state requires this. Second, it is critical that the trainer's behavior is under control and that the training environment is distraction free. If these basic conditions are not met we will not be able to understand the relationship between ourselves (as trainers) and our cats.

Training your cat is not hard but it does require some skill. Talking to others, moving about and/or eating something while trying to train a cat will only confuse him. Remember, your behavior sends a message. This message should be simple and clear: To project the message it is necessary to have control of the environment, control of consequences for behavior, and control of our own behavior.

*Remember, cats are also skilled at sending messages.*

## STIMULUS

A stimulus is something that evokes behavior. Listed below are some typical stimuli we and cats encounter in our lives that cause certain reactions.

| Stimulus | Behavior |
|---|---|
| Cold weather | Wear jacket |
| Phone rings | Got to phone and pick up receiver |
| Cat sees prey | Cat crouches, ears flatten, muscles tense |
| Sound of can opener | Cat runs to kitchen |

*From the size of this cat's paw, he has evidently received an unpleasant stimulus.*

A stimulus can be anything that affects our senses. It acquires power to affect a behavior when it is associated with consequences. These consequences are either *reinforcing* (pleasant, nice, wonderful, all inferred states), *neutral* (nothing either good or bad occurs in their presence) or *punishing* (unpleasant, painful).

You, as a stimulus, have probably acquired certain reinforcing properties that affect your cat's behavior.

*The most effective stimulus is food or the promise of it.*

To the cat you're associated with petting, feeding and shelter. When you call your cat, "Here, Nutley, here, kitty, kitty," your voice is heard by Nutley and he behaves in a predictable manner by making tracks for home. Your call has been associated with the presence of food. It is also noteworthy that the other cats within earshot don't come running to you when you call and that Nutley doesn't react when he hears a neighbor call "Here, kitty, kitty." These very real possibilities don't occur because Nutley and other cats make what is called a *stimulus discrimination*, that is, your voice as a stimulus can be recognized among other voices. This happens because your voice has been paired in the past with food, whereas other voices (those of your neighbors) have not. Your voice, as a stimulus has come to exert some control over Nutley. When it comes to do so in a reliable manner you have acquired *"stimulus control"* over Nutley's behavior.

## REINFORCEMENT

Reinforcement is a technical term used by behavioral psychologists to describe an event or condition that follows a response which increases the probability of that response occurring again. The word "reward" comes closest to describing reinforcement; a reward, however, is something that gives pleasure, and cats differ as to what they find pleasurable. Primarily the reinforcer used will consist of giving the cat something to eat in return for certain responses. The piece of food reinforces the cat for making those responses.

*Food is not only the most effective stimulus but the most effective reinforcement.*

If, afterwards, the cat performs these acts more frequently, reinforcement is occurring. Let's look at some behaviors your cat probably makes now and identify what reinforcement is occurring.

| Behavorial Responses | Reinforcement |
| --- | --- |
| Cat sits nearby when you eat | Cat gets scrap of food |
| Cat jumps on your lap | Cat is scratched under chin |
| Cat lies in sunny spot | Cat is warmed |
| Cat rubs against your leg | Cat is fed |
| Cat paws at door | Cat is let out |

The results of behavior shape behavior and are necessary to understand it. By managing what follows behavior we can control it. Indeed, a case can be made that behavior is a function of its consequences.

## GENERALIZATION

Generalization is important because it helps us to understand why Mi-Mi responds predictably by performing her trick in one situation but not in others. Those stimuli (the signals, trainer, room, smell of food, and

*You can change tricks by changing props.*

25

so forth) that were associated with the trick and the resulting reinforcement come to control Mi-Mi's behavior. Generalization occurs when Mi-Mi responds in a similar manner to different stimuli.

Mi-Mi's trick will not automatically occur in settings other than the one where it was learned. Stimulus control with cats appears to be tight. The stimuli present when reinforcement occurs control the behavior.

*Here is another example of changing a trick.*

The more identical the stimulus, the more likely the behavior is to occur. Same trainer, same room, same props, same time, same treats, location for trainer and furniture—trick is performed.

Change one or two of these conditions, and it may not be, especially if the condition is the trainer, room or props. You can't expect Mi-Mi to perform well before floodlights, flashbulbs, and a thousand screaming children. These stimuli were not present when she learned the tricks.

*In time, a cat will perform with a different person, but it takes patience.*

If you want your cat to exhibit his repertoire of tricks under a variety of conditions you should take this problem of generalization into account. Alter only one or two elements of the original training situation at a time. Take it in small steps.

Two kinds of generalization that you might want to occur are: 1) The cat will perform the trick at the command of another person; and 2) The cat will perform

*The more complicated the changes, the more time and patience are required (especially by the cat).*

his trick at a location different from where it was learned. If you want your cat to perform under the direction of a new person, it is suggested that you have that person stand next to the trainer while the trainer has the cat do the trick. The new person should then reinforce the cat with a treat. Do this a couple of times, then have the individual give the cues for the trick in a similar manner to that of the trainer.

Sometimes, a trick can be generalized to a new room or location on the first try if the cat is hungry and the trainer gives the cues in a precise manner. However, you probably will need to be a bit more patient and give the cues several times. If this doesn't work, it is recommended that you have the cat perform the trick where it was first learned and then gradually start having the trick performed several feet closer to the new location on each successive try.

*Cats when properly reinforced are much more patient than people think.*

## SIGNALS

Signals are used to give information to the cat to perform the trick and also during the initial training to ensure that the response we want the cat to make is made. There are three types of signal: verbal, hand, and physical. A verbal signal consists of giving the cat a verbal cue. For example, if the cat is being taught to lie down, the trainer should say "down" as he pushes the cat to a down position.

A hand signal consists of pointing or making a motion with the hand while providing the verbal command. With the trick "down," this consists of partially extending the hand with the elbow bent and the palm

of the hand open towards the cat. This hand signal, paired with the command provides more information than either alone would.

Physical signals are sometimes needed during the early training period of a trick. They consist of the trainer physically handling the cat. In teaching the cat to lie down, the trainer physically pushes the cat off its feet while he gives the command "down."

By the effective use of signals you create a training situation where learning can occur with a minimum of error. We want the cat to succeed, to receive reinforcement, to enjoy training. It is not necessary for the cat to make mistakes in order to learn. Indeed, a frustrated cat can be awful.

## FADING OF SIGNALS

Fading involves gradually changing the stimuli presented; to enable the cat to recognize signals other than those which he could at first. In cat training we are talking about lessening the amount of signals necessary to have the cat make a desired response. At first, it may be necessary to physically assist the cat to get the response we wish to reinforce. Or, it may be necessary to hold the edible reinforcer in a certain position relative to the cat to have him make the response. By gradually eliminating these signals (fading them), we can get to a point where the response is made without them, and your cat will perform that trick given only the verbal and hand signal.

# Training Tips

1. *Do training before meals when the cat is hungry.*
Training will be less effective if your cat is well fed. A
well-fed cat is a lazy cat. Your cat will look at you with
a look that says "You must be joking!"

*"Who, me?
Jump through
that?"*

**2.** *Conduct training in a distraction-free environment.* Remove other pets. Remove your family. Not only will they distract the cat, but they will probably get on your nerves, too. If other people insist that they simply must watch, ask them to sit still, not chat, offer advice, or comment on the cat's performance. In other

*This is not what the author meant by a "distraction-free environment." Try to avoid this sort of thing until your cat is well trained.*

words, discourage them—at worst, you might try telling them that some cats under the stress of training have been known to go berserk and attack bystanders.

3. *Find an effective reinforcer.* Not all cats like the same thing. You'll know it if you're understanding. Meowing and climbing up the walls are good signs. Reinforcement should be something that you can easily hold in your hand and deliver in small portions. If your cat normally eats a dried food or one of the bite-sized moistened foods, these are ideal. *A note of caution:* If your cat has been on a steady diet of dried food it is recommended that initially you take it easy with the moist foods. Your cat may love it but he may also "chuck it."

*In this case, the reinforcement is in the glass and a part of the trick.*

**4.** *Give reinforcement immediately after trick is performed.* The behavior that occurred most immediately before reinforcement is most heavily retained. This means that if your cat performs a trick, then proceeds to turn around three times and rub against your leg before you deliver the reinforcer, the turning around and leg rubbing has been reinforced and your cat may start to exhibit these behaviors as part of the trick. If you like it, keep it in the act by reinforcing it. If you don't, be careful not to reinforce it.

*If your cats are trained separately in the same location, you can eventually get them to perform together.*

*Do not reinforce
your cat too
often or too
heavily.*

5. *After your cat has mastered a trick, stop reinforcing him each time he does it.* Start reinforcing kitty on a more random schedule. While the cat is being taught to perform the trick, reinforcing him each time he does it is most effective. However, once the trick is learned, reinforcing him randomly (sometimes after one time, sometimes after two or three) will have the effect of causing the trick to become a more permanent feature of the cat's behavioral repertoire. This seems odd; but it works.

6. *Give your hand signal distinctly.* Hold still before giving the signal. You want it to stand out. You don't want it to occur in the clutter of other movements.

You are sending signals to your cat. Think of it as semaphore; do it cleanly and crisply and the transmitted message is more apt to be read.

7. *Give verbal command clearly and distinctly.* Everything said with regard to hand signals applies equally to verbal ones. Don't talk excessively to the cat . . . "Come on now, Dexter, Dexter, jump, come on now, kitty, kitty, jump." Your cat will resent it. You may feel better; but Dexter won't. Keep the message simple.

8. *Before giving command* "roll," "jump," etc., *say the cat's name.* Say it clearly. Try to achieve eye contact with your cat when saying his name, then immediately pair it with the commands for the trick and the hand signals.

9. *Make sure cat succeeds at least seventy-five percent of the time.* If your cat isn't succeeding, the task requirements are too high. Go back to an earlier training step for the trick. Cats need success (just as we do) and will evidence frustration if not reinforced.

10. *Stop a training session on an upbeat note.* Don't wait until your cat gets filled up with reinforcers. Well-fed cats don't care about being cute or clever. As mentioned earlier, they are lazy. Stop the training after your cat has done particularly well at performing the trick or training step of a trick. Give several treats to that fantastic cat. He will associate training with good times.

11. *Avoid physically shaping new behavior with the cat if at all possible.* With the scent of food reinforcers in the air the cat is apt to be a bit tense. This is not to say that physical shaping can't be done, but as a general rule it is better to figure out how to get the response from the cat *without* touching. (Touching kitty when he's tense can result in ugliness.)

12. *Think of this training as a dance.* You are whistling the tune and you are leading. Be as sensitive as you can about your behavior and the cat's. See the cause-effect relationships. See responses to almost every movement and sound you make. Watch the ears—nothing is missed. Input-output. Cause and

effect. There is music and art here. By attending to it you'll be a better trainer.

13. *Teach your cat only one trick at a time.* Once a trick is well-established, you can train your cat to perform a new trick without fear that the first one will be lost in the process.

# Why Rapid Learning Occurs

1. Cat is taught in distraction-free setting. Other stimuli do not compete for cat's attention and interfere with learning.

2. Immediate reinforcement for desired stunt occurs. The cat receives accurate and timely feedback.

3. Frequent repetition of task facilitates learning. Practice makes perfect.

4. Training objectives are concrete. We know what we want and can see whether we are successful or not. We are not engaged in some vague exercise such as developing our cat to its fullest potential or broadening its horizons. All we ask is for Nutley to sit on the stool when we say "sit" and give the correct hand signal. It either happens or it doesn't. If it doesn't happen the first or second time, we'll get over it. It might take a while, but we'll get over it.

5. Tricks are taught in easily achievable steps. We are operating at a cat's level of ability based on observable behavior—not asking too much.

# TRICKS

# Sit

**TRICK**. Cat will go to specified location: chair, stool, or prop, such as a wagon or a toy truck, and sit when the trainer gives the signal.

## MATERIALS

1. Cat—one of average intelligence.
2. Trainer—one with a willingness to learn.
3. Sitting platform—use your imagination, but don't overdo it. The refrigerator is not a good idea.
4. Bite-sized reinforcers.
5. A quiet location for training.


## COMMENTS

This trick is an excellent starting point for shaping up your cat's behavior. It is a good first lesson for the trainer, too. It will give you experience at practicing the basic training techniques; giving verbal and hand signals, fading of signals, and reinforcing kitty. With any luck at all, *you* will be reinforced by kitty rapidly acquiring this trick. Nothing succeeds like success. You will gain confidence in your ability to train your cat and proceed to more impressive tricks.

If you are not successful in teaching your cat this simple stunt it is possible that you or your cat (or both) are not capable of mastering this art. However, don't give up too soon; your trouble may be that you are overanxious and are not keeping your own behavior under tight control, which would affect your cat. Relax; review training techniques. Do not lose confidence in yourself or your cat (who probably still has confidence in you). Leave it alone for a few days then try again. You might (if one is available) try teaching another cat.

*Step 2.*

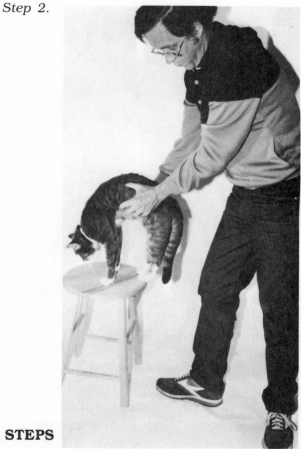

## TRAINING STEPS

1. Decide where you'd like the cat to sit when you give verbal and hand signals. Any item that kitty will look great sitting in or on will be fine. The only requirement is that your cat has easy access. We'll assume you decide to use a small stool as the prop for sitting. 2. Place reinforcers in your hand, and place the cat several feet from the stool. Stand near the stool and

say "_____, sit." Give an extended arm point towards stool; then pick up your cat and place him on the stool. Immediately reinforce your cat. As he completes eating the reinforcer and looks up, give him a second treat, then step back several paces. Stand perfectly still and stare at kitty. Don't talk to him (or yourself), don't move, just maintain your stare. Your cat will probably remain sitting on the stool for several seconds. After all, it isn't such a bad place to sit! Do nothing, say nothing, watch cat. Do not distract him.

3. Repeat step #2 a couple of times. After the second time, wait for your cat to leave the stool, then proceed to step #4.

4. After your cat leaves the stool and has moved several feet from it, wait a few seconds, then say "_____, sit." When you say this, give an arm point towards the

stool. Wait for the cat to obey. Maintain your pose and let 15–30 seconds elapse. If the cat hasn't gone over to the stool and jumped on it, drop your arm, wait a few seconds, then repeat command and signal. If your cat goes to the stool and sits on it, immediately reinforce him—heavily, with lots of praise and treats.

*Step 4.*

If your cat doesn't sit on the stool after being given two or three commands/points, do the following: Give the command and point. Then go to the stool and tap your finger on it, saying "sit" as you do so. If necessary, hold the reinforcer above the stool to entice the cat to jump on it. When he does, reinforce him.

5. If you're having trouble getting your cat to respond to the command and point, repeat step #2 two or

three times. Then proceed to step #3. *Remember, when you give commands and gestures, give them clearly and distinctly. We're talking theatre. You want a clear, simple message sent to the cat.*
6. Once your cat is responding well to verbal and gestural signals you can start placing yourself farther from the stool before giving them.

## SUMMARY

Unless your cat is unusual, he should learn this trick rather quickly. In the event kitty is slow or obstinate, be patient. Once your cat learns that he'll be fed if he sits on the stool he'll quickly go there. This trick is very similar to the situation mentioned earlier where the sound of the can opener served as a stimulus for your cat to run into the kitchen. Substitute your voice saying "sit" and the signal for the stimulus of the can-opener sound, and the similarity is complete. In all probability, after a few learning trials, your pet will be sitting on the stool on his own.

As you gain some control over your cat (this is fantastic, isn't it?) you may want him to be under the more precise control of your voice and the signal. To do this, start withholding reinforcement for "sitting" on his own. Reinforce only "sitting" that occurs after *you* have directed him to sit. Also, to encourage this you can occasionally reinforce the cat for just "hanging around." Then give the cues and reinforce the cat for "sitting."

# Up

**TRICK**. Cat will sit like a groundhog (up on back legs with front paws up) when you give verbal and hand signals.

## MATERIALS

1. A cat whose mother was a groundhog.
2. A platform to "show off" on.
3. Reinforcers.
4. A small whip and chair for the trainer. This will greatly enhance the dramatic effect of "up."

## HAND SIGNAL

A thumbs up (the hitchhiker's sign).

## COMMENTS

"Up" is an extremely easy trick to teach your cat. All you need to do is get him to assume a groundhog position so that you can reinforce it. Physically shaping it, showing the cat pictures of groundhogs, and describing the posture to him won't work. Follow the training steps shown here and you'll encounter no problems. Your cat will be "up" in no time at all and you'll be the proud owner of a cat that can masquerade as a groundhog.

*Steps 1 and 2.*

## TRAINING STEPS

1. Select a place for kitty to act like he's a groundhog. Perhaps where he learned to go when you taught him "sit" would be a good location. Or, get a plastic laundry basket. Kitty can pretend he's peeking out of his den, looking for predators.
2. Train kitty to go to location for exhibiting trick using the training steps for the trick "sit."

3. With kitty at location, give verbal command "up." Pair this command with hand signal and hold reinforcer above the cat. Your cat will stand on his hind legs or haunches and attempt to knock it out of your hand. Be careful. When your cat is "up" in a satisfactory manner, say "good, _____" and reinforce him. Do

*Step 3.*

*Step 3.*

this several trials. If you experience difficulties getting kitty into an "up" position, you can achieve the same ends by dangling a string tied to a short stick above him when you give the prompts.

4. Fade out the holding of reinforcer (or string) above your cat while at the same time holding the verbal and

hand signals. At each successive trial, move several inches from the cat until you can have him perform the trick while you stand several feet away.

## SUMMARY

That wasn't so hard now, was it? The only aspect of the trick that required skill was the fading of the signals used to get kitty in an "up" position. The most important aspect of this trick was in getting the desired response without the need to physically shape it.

# Down

**Trick**. Cat will lie down with feet out from under himself when verbal and hand signals are given.

## MATERIALS

1. Cooperative cat. If being touched when not in the mood angers your cat you should skip this trick. You don't want to struggle with kitty.
2. A well-stocked medicine cabinet. You may get hurt if the above warning is not heeded.
3. Reinforcers. Your cat isn't going to get "down" without them any quicker than you'd go to work without promise of pay.

## HAND SIGNAL

Flex your elbow tightly with your arm near your body and present an open palm towards the cat.

## COMMENTS

Some cats learn this trick very rapidly, others don't. The primary obstacle to teaching this trick is the need for the trainer to physically shape this stunt. Unlike the previous trick, "sit," in which we were able to get the cat to perform with little physical intervention, this trick requires the trainer to physically push kitty off his feet and onto his side. Most cats don't object to this, they'll acquire "down" in no time at all. Other cats dislike being pushed off their feet. However, with patience and gentleness you should succeed. Another potential problem area with this trick is that it requires a greater degree of sensitivity on the trainer's part because of the need to fade-out the physical prompt. This, in fact, is the trick.

## TRAINING STEPS

1. Say "_____, down" with arm gesture. Immediately after command, gently push your cat down and off his feet. As you push him down, repeat command quietly but distinctly, "down, down." As soon as the cat is completely on his side with his feet out, reinforce with several tasty morsels.

When pushing the cat down, be aware of his resistance. Do no more pushing than necessary. If kitty is lowering himself, stop the physical push. When the cat stops the movement to lie down, give a gentle push.

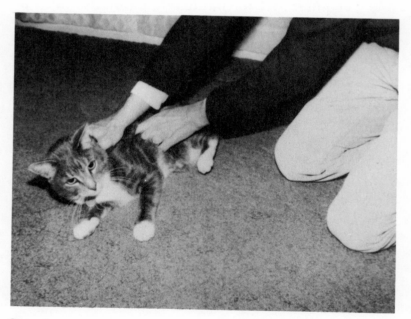

*Step 1.*

During the teaching of this trick, if you need to touch your cat to evoke a downward movement, keep your hand on, or just over him, until he is completely lying down (no arm and hand movements in and out from your body towards it). Also, during initial physical pushing, kitty may get upset and attempt to flee. Once you start a physical push don't let your cat loose. Be gentle and smooth, don't startle him. Once kitty is "down," reinforce heavily.

2. Do step #1 several times. After six or seven trials you should be noticing less resistance from your cat to physical prompting. As this resistance lessens, you can taper off the amount of reinforcement.

3. When your cat is lying down with only a slight touch required, try to eliminate the physical push altogether. Give command "down" paired with hand signal. Move your hand towards kitty as though you were going to physically push, but stop short of touching him. Hold pose. Wait and see if he will lie down. If he squats, gently push him onto his side and reinforce. If he doesn't squat or lie down, do nothing, just hold your position. Let him either lie down and be reinforced or do nothing and consequently, receive nothing. You call the shots.

4. When kitty goes down without being touched, start holding back your hand. Where earlier you may have had to merely touch kitty to get the response, start now to move your hand towards him only to the smallest extent necessary to get the response. Once you get to the point where you don't have to touch the cat to have him lie down, you are "home free."

*Step 3.*

5. Once kitty lies down with little physical prompting, go for broke. Simply give the command and gesture. Stare at him, but don't move; see what he does. Comment: If kitty stares at you, cocks his head to one side or walks in circles, you're in luck. Wait. Repeat command and gesture if kitty does not appear to be on the verge of lying down. (I repeat: *cocking head and circling are good signs.*)

# SUMMARY

Some cats learn "down" in ten or less trials. Others may need many more. The skill of the trainer in correctly assessing how much the cat will do independently and using this as a basis for how much physical prompting is necessary is one of the more important variables which influence the required training time. The other critical variable is your cat. If your cat is tactically defensive, training will require more skill (and perhaps a good knowledge of first aid).

# Roll

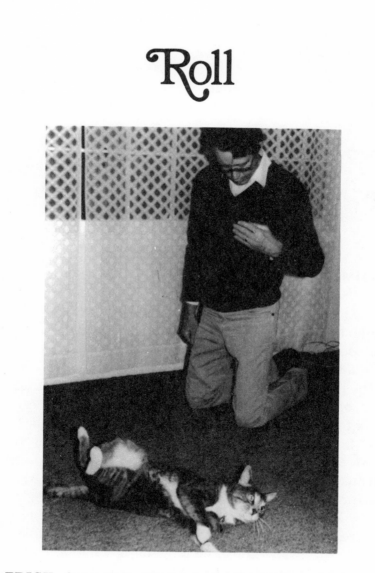

**TRICK**. Cat will lie down and roll to his opposite side
when trainer gives verbal and hand signal.

## MATERIALS

1. A cat that likes to hang around the dinner table.
2. Reinforcers for cat.
3. Reinforcers for trainer.

## HAND SIGNAL

Place your hand over your heart and rotate it (your hand, not your heart).

## COMMENTS

The trick "down" is a prerequisite for "roll." If it weren't, we'd be talking "flip." Flip is not covered in this book. Cats have built-in gyroscopes that prevent this action.

"Roll" is a good trick for your cat to learn. It requires no props and can be performed anywhere. It is an easy trick for him to perform. He does it all of the time. I'll bet that when your cat sees you arrive at home he drops to the pavement or floor and rolls. He's yawning because he's been sleeping all day while you've been slaving away.

The life of a loved cat is hard. His day is filled with leisure, stalking, sleep and wild fantasies. This takes its toll—just having fun all day, doing what you want to do—it's an empty life. No wonder kitty perks up and rolls when you come home. A cat needs some comedy relief, and your return signals some. Poor kitty has been forced to "make do" all day on his own. Too much sleep and pleasure have tired him. Now he has you and can be a passive observer of the insane world of human beings. He just prays that you don't blow his furry hide off the face of the earth along with yours and spoil this delightful routine.

## TRAINING STEPS

1. Stare at kitty. Say, "down" as you give the hand signal. As soon as the cat is down, say "roll," dragging out the pronunciation to "rooolll." Immediately take your hand and gently roll him onto his back and onto his other side. You may find that you can get your cat to make this maneuver by holding the treat in front of his face and then moving it to his opposite side. The cat, in moving his head to track the treat, will roll over. Another tactic that sometimes accomplishes this is to simply drop the reinforcer on the floor on the opposite side of the cat after he has laid down as you say "roll." Three approaches have been suggested for getting your cat to roll: a) Manually do it. b) Kitty initiates maneuver in order to visually track reinforcer. c) Kitty initiates move to eat treat.

Each cat has its own personality, and it is difficult to give a pat prescription for which approach to use. What works well for one cat may not for another. However, here are some things to consider. If your cat, in mastering "down" didn't struggle or attempt to flee when being pushed down physically, he probably

won't mind being rolled physically. The advantage to this technique is that it is easy to pair in a tight sequence the stimulus ("roll") and the response (rolling). Its disadvantage lies in the necessity of having to fade-out the physical prompt.

The advantage of getting the cat to roll by having kitty watch the reinforcer is that this signal lends itself to fading more easily than the physical prompt.

*Step 2.*

Sometimes combining visual tracking with a little assist from your hand works well. The merit of simply dropping the treat to the opposite side of the cat when he is down, to get him to roll, is in the ease of fading out this gesture and the food-drop. All that is required is to lessen the amount dropped and to praise and reinforce when the roll is completed. After you have

dropped the reinforcer two or three times you can virtually stop dropping anything. The cat will see the arm movement and will check things out. He'll think "did I miss something" and will roll over to see; after all, that arm movement and command previously resulted in a treat. The disadvantage of this technique is the distinct possibility that the cat won't roll to get the reinforcer but will simply stand up and eat it. This does not make for a very impressive trick.

2. After you've conducted ten to twenty trials of step #1 give the command and gesture and wait kitty out. Just stare at him and wait. Don't move. The cat will be lying there staring back at you, waiting. You are to wait longer than he. If the cat starts to roll, but then hesitates, immediately give a light physical push, to complete the roll. Then reinforce. If kitty rolls completely on his own after the stare-down, you have succeeded. Heavily reinforce both the cat and yourself. If you have been observant while shaping the cat's behavior you should have some feel for how dependent your cat is on you for prompts or physical intervention.

If you believe your cat is close to initiating the move then try the command and stare. It can't do any harm. Also, if you simply don't know if kitty has learned anything, give it a shot. You might be pleasantly surprised. Of course, you also might be sadly disappointed.

3. If kitty completed the roll with a slight push, attempt to lessen this with each successive trial. On occasion, do the "stare and wait" routine.

4. Once your cat is rolling with you nearby, gradually start moving farther away from kitty when you give the command and gesture. Also, if you want, you can give the command "roll" right at the start of the trick. It won't matter to kitty whether you say "down" or "roll." Ninety-five percent of the information he is receiving says "roll."

## ADDITIONAL COMMENTS

If you want your cat to make the distinction between "down" and "roll," the following thoughts are offered:

1. It is difficult, and it may not be worth the effort.

2. You can achieve the same end in appearance by conducting the tricks "down" and "roll" in different settings. The stimulus control of that environment will control whether kitty rolls or lies down. It may appear that kitty is a brilliant scholar and is responding appropriately to verbal command but this is not the case. To prove the point say "turkey" as opposed to "roll" and see if the cat doesn't roll. Now, if you're really serious about this business—and after all, what makes a trick a trick is behavior under precise stimulus control—then, when you say "down" and "roll" make the words sound as different as possible. Perhaps say "down" curtly and say "roll" all dragged out. The more different the sound the easier to tell them apart.

3. After giving the command "down," reinforce your cat for lying down immediately. Then gradually delay reinforcement. If kitty takes delay in reinforcement as a discriminative event to do something more—such as roll—and subsequently does so, do not reinforce.

## SUMMARY

Of all the tricks presented in this book, "roll" may be the most difficult from a training standpoint. The trainer's skill in figuring out to what degree the cat is dependent on him for prompts is crucial. If your cat learned "down" he can learn "roll." Between the cat and yourself, there is sufficient talent.

# Through the Hoop

**TRICK**. Cat will jump through a hoop held between platforms when given a hand signal and command such as "jump, fool." (Actually a simple "jump" will do.)

## MATERIALS

1. A hungry cat.
2. Platforms, i.e., chairs, stools, boxes, anything that kitty can get a grip on that won't tip over and scare the jabbers out of him.
3. A hoop. One about fourteen inches in diameter works well for all sizes of cats except the fattest, and they aren't going to fly far anyway. You can use any item you want, i.e., bicycle wheel rim, or knitting frame, as long as it resembles a hoop.
4. Bite-sized reinforcers.
5. A distraction-free environment. No other cats around. No excited onlookers. No "doubting Thomases." No music; although the theme song from *Born Free* is acceptable.

## COMMENTS

When one thinks of Bengal tigers performing at the circus, this is the trick that one remembers. Power, grace, coordination, and a flaming hoop. Terrific! Your cat can do this, too. However, it is recommended that you dispense with the fire. The smell of burnt fur is highly offensive. Also, your insurance company may not cover the cost of replacing your home when they discover that the fire was started by a household cat jumping through a flaming hoop in the living room. They may even think you're an idiot.

This trick is surprisingly easy for a cat to learn. It's as easy as "sit"; nothing to it. Chairs make excellent launching and landing sites. Or, if you have some stools that won't tip over as kitty blasts off into space, they'll work fine too.

*Mission Control recommends the following training steps:*

## TRAINING STEPS

1. Place chairs (or whatever) several inches apart. Your cat should be able to easily step across the gap between them.
2. Put reinforcer in right hand. Hold hoop in your left hand, between the chairs, with its bottom edge at the same level as the chair seats. If you're left-handed do it the other way around—it doesn't matter.

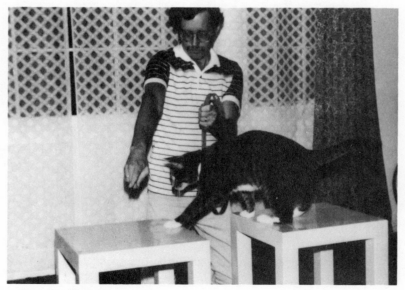

Steps 1 and 2.

*Note how tables are moved slightly farther apart than in first photo.*

3. Direct or entice kitty with a treat to gain a chair seat for himself. If your cat learned "sit" on the prop you're using you are a step ahead in this game.

4. While holding the hoop in one hand, give a full arm point to the empty chair with your opposite hand. Say "jump," then hold the treat in front of kitty and lead him across the gap between the chairs and through the hoop. Give him a reinforcer. Do this two or three times.

5. Move the chairs a little farther apart. Give verbal and hand signal. See kitty go. Reinforce kitty with a treat. Do this several times at a distance that just

*Here the hoop is lifted higher.*

*And, in this step, the hoop is higher still.*

barely requires your cat to jump. After doing this successfully six or seven times you should be at a stage of training where you don't need to hold the treat in view of your cat, so don't. Simply give command and point.

6. As the cat gets into the act of jumping to and fro, space the chairs farther apart and raise the hoop higher. There's nothing to this trick.

## SUMMARY

Very quickly, the hoop and chairs will become the discriminative stimuli for performing this trick. Your cat will jump without command or hand signal. Just stand there like an idiot with the hoop between the chairs, and he'll know what to do. You won't even need a whip.

At some point, as you ask more of your cat by placing the chairs farther apart and the hoop higher, kitty will decide there is an easier way to do this. Clever kitty will decide that going through the hoop needn't be part of the trick. He'll simply step off the chair and walk over to the other chair, jump onto it and look for

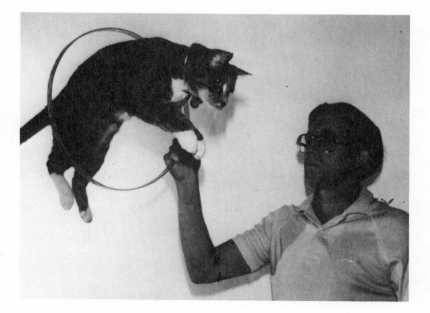

his treat. Jumping is a bore. When your lazy cat steps off the chair to do it this way, say "no." Say it matter-of-factly and turn your head away from him and re-move the hoop. Ignore the cat, just stand still. Your cat will return to his chair. (Note: Cat will develop right-to-left or left-to-right jump preference unless you exercise care to see that he has equal success and hence, reinforcement for each direction.)

Your cat will perform best at the start of training sessions. Once the trick is learned he'll make the most spectacular jumps during initial trials. When you show off your animal to a guest by having him do the hoop trick, do the initial jump at a medium distance. Then go for the gold!

# Drink Trick

**TRICK**. Cat will place his paw in a glass of liquid when the trainer says "glass" and gives hand signal.

## MATERIALS

1. A fun-loving cat.
2. A trainer who can go along with a joke.
3. A glass containing liquid. The glass must be wide enough for the cat to stick his paw in it; and short enough for him not to tip it over when he does.

## HAND SIGNAL

An extended arm point.

## COMMENTS

This is a popular trick for kitty. When you have guests at your home and kitty places his paw in someone's drink he will impress everyone. To be able to order your cat to do something so alien to his nature surprises people.

While at first glance, this trick may appear to be a rather difficult trick to teach a cat because of its well-known dislike to getting wet, it is, in fact, really quite simple. The essence of it lies in figuring out how to get kitty to put his paw in a glass. There are only two methods for achieving this end. One, you can physically shape it; that is physically put the cat's paw in the glass for him. Or, you can set up a situation where kitty will put his paw in the glass by himself. Unless you enjoy pain, I suggest the last method. Give kitty a reason to put his paw in the glass by putting some food in it. You know this will work. As you've learned, he always investigates anything that looks edible. Certainly he'll fish around in a glass for a delicious treat. You are now ninety percent of the way home with this trick. The last steps are fairly easy.

*Step 1.*

## TRAINING STEPS

1. Place an empty glass on the coffee table or whatever place you've selected for the trick to be performed.
2. Allow your cat to smell the reinforcers in your hand. Then, with him watching, point directly down into the glass and say "glass" as you drop a treat into it. When the cat puts his paw into the glass to fish out the treat, say "good, _____ " and place a reinforcer beside the glass.

If your cat is so engrossed in getting the treat out of the glass that he doesn't attend to the reinforcer, allow him to complete his task, then immediately give it to him. Repeat this sequence several times (giving a verbal and hand signal, coupled with dropping the treat into the glass, followed by reinforcement for placing his paw in the glass).

By following this routine you'll create a situation where the placing of the treat into the glass acts as a signal to cause the behavior your cat is being reinforced for. After a number of times he will become less dependent on the treat in the glass as a cause for exhibiting this. behavior.

3. Fade out the dropping of treat into glass. Do so by dropping less treat on each successive trial. Maintain the verbal and hand signals while doing so. The stimulus complex that is being paired with the desired behavior, and subsequent reinforcement will play a greater role in controlling the behavior. After a few successful trials of fading out the prompt (edible in glass), attempt a trial with no treat being dropped. (A little sleight of hand is good for your cat. After all, he's put a

few "fast ones" over on you on more than one occasion.) If kitty places his paw into the glass, reinforce him. If he doesn't, storm out of the room in a tantrum. Once you've vented your frustration you'll feel better and will be able to return to the training session (as calm and as cool as the cat) to conduct a few more fading trials with the treat.

4. Once your cat puts his paw into the glass without the treat being present, start fading out the presence of your hand over the glass. With each successive trial, move your hand away from the glass several inches until you can deliver the hand and verbal signal from several feet away.

*Step 4.*

5. Put about one-half inch of liquid in the glass. Deliver signals. When kitty puts his paw in the glass and touches the liquid, reinforce him. By this time you can probably just stand nearby and he'll repeatedly

place his paw into the glass and look towards you for his reinforcer. Very quickly you'll have a wet area around the glass and a cat that is becoming quite casual about liquid.

6. There are several kinds of generalizations that you may want to occur. Perhaps it would be clever if kitty "did his thing" with other liquids in the glass, or with different sized glasses, or at other locations than where the trick was learned, or with other people nearby. If you wish to pursue any of these avenues, select one and gradually introduce it. Other liquids will be easy as long as you don't change the glass or where the glass was sitting when the trick was

learned. Having the stunt performed at a different location poses no problem if you minimize any distractions and use the same glass.

Introducing people and noise while the trick is being performed is more difficult. Start by having the cat do the trick with the stereo on. Then have the trick performed with music on and one other person present. Next, chat with this person; tell a few jokes and laugh while the stereo is on and have your cat perform. Now, have the neighbors and friends come over and offer them drinks—you and your cat's reputation is assured.


## SUMMARY

The training procedure used with this trick is a good example of the technique of getting the desired behavior to occur "naturally" so that we can reinforce it and acquire stimulus control over it. Physically shaping the desired response in this situation would be very difficult. Yet by manipulating the cat's environment, the behavior can be achieved very easily. This principle can be applied to other tricks you might want to teach your cat. If you can get him to exhibit a behavior on his own, you can pair it with other specific stimuli (such as signals), reinforce it, and thereby acquire control over its occurrence.

# Epilogue

# People and Cats

Has training your cat to be a performing artist through the use of behavior modification in any way lessened the mystery surrounding him? Has he been reduced to a mindless automaton by our acquiring a degree of insight into the role of environmental stimuli and reinforcement in shaping and maintaining behavior?

Turn your attention to your cat, gaze upon him, and decide for yourself. There he lies in all his cold indifference; close but distant, mind in space, body on the radiator soaking up heat; an enigma cloaked in a cocoon of hedonistic self-interest. A riddle of contentment and independence, yet soft and cuddly, he still retains that nebulous look in his eyes too! Heaven knows, he could awaken at any moment and behave in a manner far beyond the reach of any learning theories to describe in cause-effect relationships.

There still remains a goodly part of Cat that is beyond our understanding. He may have indulged us in some of our follies by jumping through the hoop when his needs could be met, but he remains uniquely a cat. He may even believe in his own way that he has *us* trained to give him food when he gives specific signals.

# Index